For Eileen, who said, "It could be a
book!" — with love and gratitude.
— J.B.

For my father and brother who, like
Georgia, made being adventurous
look effortless. — B.A.

Text © 2005 by Jen Bryant
Illustrations © 2005 by Bethanne Andersen
Published 2005 by Eerdmans Books for Young Readers
An imprint of Wm. B. Eerdmans Publishing Company
2140 Oak Industrial Dr. NE, Grand Rapids, Michigan 49505
P.O. Box 163, Cambridge CB3 9PU U.K.

*www.eerdmans.com/youngreaders*

Manufactured at Tien Wah Press in Singapore in November 2009, 3rd printing

10  11  12  13  14  15  16    9  8  7  6  5  4  3

**Library of Congress Cataloging-in-Publication Data**

Bryant, Jennifer.
Georgia's bones / written by Jen Bryant ; illustrated by Bethanne Andersen.— 1st ed.
p. cm.
Summary: Artist Georgia O'Keeffe was interested in the shapes she saw
around her, from her childhood on a Wisconsin farm to her adult life in
New York City and New Mexico.
ISBN 978-0-8028-5217-5 (cloth : alk. paper)
ISBN 978-0-8028-5367-7 (pbk : alk. paper)
1. O'Keeffe, Georgia, 1887-1986—Juvenile fiction. [1. O'Keeffe, Georgia,
1887-1986—Fiction. 2. Shape—Fiction. 3. Artists—Fiction.]
I. Andersen, Bethanne, ill. II. Title.
PZ7.B8393Ge 2005
[E]—dc22
2004006800

The display type is set in Saxophone.
The text type is set in Saxophone and Times.
The illustrations were created with gouache, colored pencil,
and pastel on Arches buff printmaking paper.

As a child, shapes often drifted
in and out of Georgia's mind.
Curved and straight, round or square,
she studied them, and let them disappear.

In the woods around her father's Wisconsin farm,
she collected shapes: flowers, leaves,
sticks and stones. She put them
in her pocket and took them home.

"Such common objects," said her brother.
"Why do you bother?" asked her sister.
"Because they please me," Georgia replied.

Spaces pleased Georgia, too —
windows and doors, dents and holes,
places she could see into or through.

When her mother made donuts,
her brothers and sisters gobbled them down
as fast as they could. But Georgia
nibbled the outside all the way around,
saving the perfect circle in the middle
for last.

"More of Georgia's silly notions," said her mother.
But Georgia didn't care.
"Someday, I'm going to be an artist," she declared.

And that's exactly what she did.
When Georgia grew up, she moved to New York City
and rented a studio on the top floor.
From her window, she saw many different shapes:
tall and thin, short and fat, round and square.
She studied them, then painted them with care.

She gathered seashells by the shore,
kept them in a drawer so she could remember
the sand and the waves. On rainy days, she took them out
and looked at their shapes and spaces.
"They please me," she told her city friends.
So she painted them, too.

One day a letter came from a friend out West:
"Will you come for a visit?"
Georgia replied: "Yes!"

In New Mexico, the sky was the sea —
huge and blue — and the clouds were waves —
light and foamy — rolling slowly across it.
No two looked the same.

Georgia studied their shapes,
the puffed-up ones thick as snowbanks,
the wispy ones that swirled over the Spanish church
as if someone had painted them there
with a milk-dipped feather.

She noticed the hills and mountains,
the houses and rivers, and watched
their colors change each day as the sun
flung itself across the sky.

In the desert, she picked up the bones
of animals — of cows and horses, pigs and sheep —
put them in a sack and took them home.

She cleaned them one by one,
then held them up to the sun.
They gleamed with a white light, pure and bright,
like the sliver of moon
that crept over the mountains at night
and hung there, a perfect curve, like a rib,
over the sleeping desert.

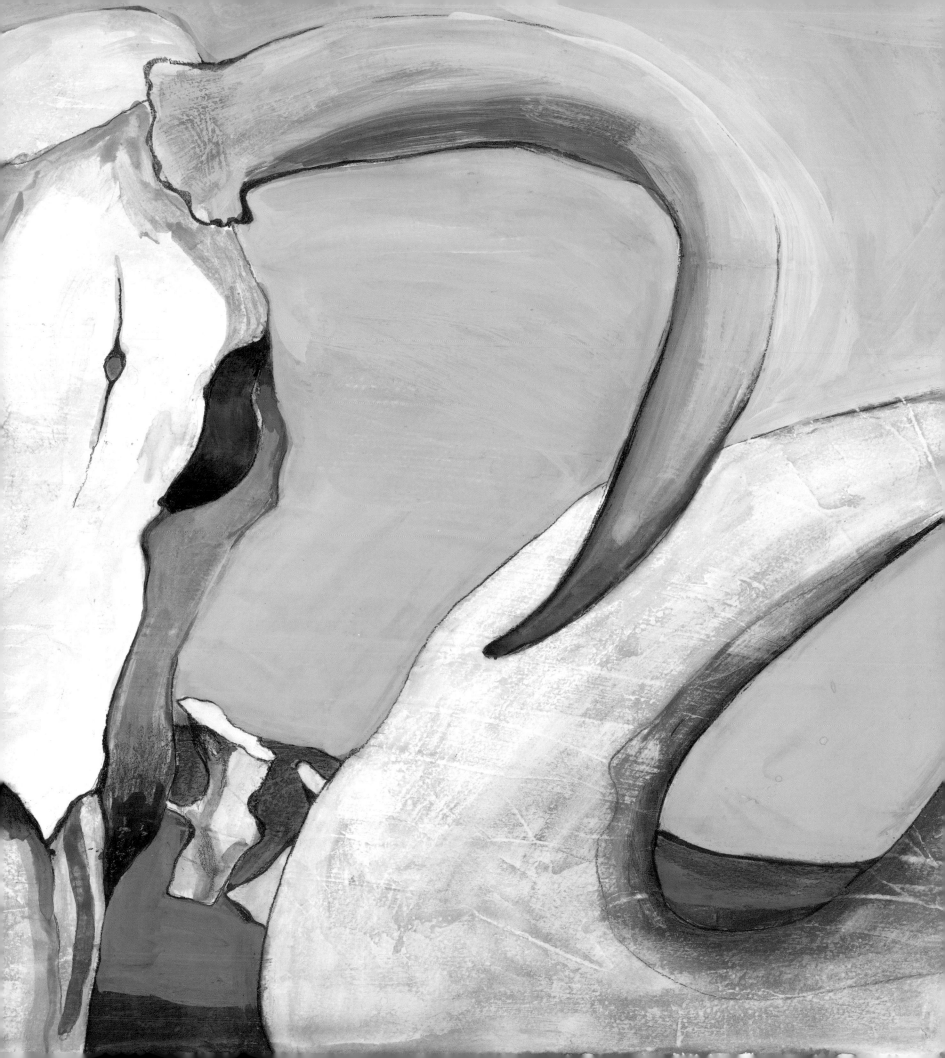

She didn't know why they pleased her so.
Perhaps it was the quiet way
they did their work — the years of being invisible,
and then, when everything fell away,
they appeared in all their purity and beauty.

Sometimes she would look at her own hand
and imagine the bones inside
doing their important work —
holding everything together.

Some bones were straight and others curved,
worn smooth by sun, wind, and sand,
a few worn so thin that when she held them up
she could see the sun through them.

The holes in the bones pleased Georgia, too.
They made frames and windows
through which she glimpsed a piece of the sky,
or a tiny corner of a mountain.

When her visit to the mountains was over,
Georgia filled a wooden barrel
with sun-bleached bones —
each one tagged and labeled —
and shipped them back to New York City.

There in her studio she took them out,
put them on a stand, where she could see them
and remember the quiet desert — the sand
and wind, the clouds and distant mountains —
and she painted them with care.